Dear Parents and Educators,

Welcome to Penguin Young Readers! As parents and educators, you know that each child develops at their own pace—in terms of speech, critical thinking, and, of course, reading. Penguin Young Readers recognizes this fact. As a result, each Penguin Young Readers book is assigned a traditional easy-to-read level (1–4) as well as an F&P Text Level (A–R). Both of these systems will help you choose the right book for your child. Please refer to the back of each book for specific leveling information. Penguin Young Readers features esteemed authors and illustrators, stories about favorite characters, fascinating nonfiction, and more!

Totally Turtles!

LEVEL 4

F&P TEXT LEVEL Q

This book is perfect for a **Fluent Reader** who:
- can read the text quickly with minimal effort;
- has good comprehension skills;
- can self-correct (can recognize when something doesn't sound right); and
- can read aloud smoothly and with expression.

Here are some **activities** you can do during and after reading this book:
- Make Connections: Some turtles, like giant tortoises on the Galápagos Islands, can live for 100 years or more. Do you know of any other animals or sea creatures that can live for that long?
- Descriptive Words: A descriptive word is one that points out a specific characteristic of someone or something. The author of this book uses a lot of descriptive words to describe the many colors, sizes, and speeds of different turtles. For example, the painted turtle has "red, orange, and yellow" shapes on its shell, the common musk turtle is described as "small," and the hawksbill sea turtle is a "fast" swimmer. Reread the book, pointing out any descriptive words you see.

Remember, sharing the love of reading with a child is the best gift you can give!

*This book has been officially leveled by using the F&P Text Level Gradient™ leveling system.

For the dedicated volunteers of NEST
(Network for Endangered Sea Turtles) in the
Outer Banks of North Carolina—GLC

PENGUIN YOUNG READERS
An imprint of Penguin Random House LLC, New York

First published in the United States of America by Penguin Young Readers,
an imprint of Penguin Random House LLC, New York, 2024

Text copyright © 2024 by Ginjer L. Clarke

Photo credits: used throughout: (photo frame) happyfoto/E+/Getty Images; cover, 3: Marnie Griffiths/
Moment/Getty Images; 4: (top) Paul Starosta/Stone/Getty Images, (bottom) CassielMx/iStock/Getty
Images; 5: (top) cturtletrax/E+/Getty Images, (bottom) pierivb/iStock/Getty Images; 6: Emirhan
Karamuk/iStock/Getty Images; 7: Kevin Schafer/The Image Bank/Getty Images; 8: Jack Reynolds/
Moment Open/Getty Images; 9: Jason Edwards/The Image Bank/Getty Images; 10: Andriy Nekrasov/
iStock/Getty Images; 11: James R.D. Scott/Moment/Getty Images; 12: Paul Souders/Stone/Getty
Images; 13: RainervonBrandis/E+/Getty Images; 14: Rawlinson_Photography/E+/Getty Images; 15:
Doug Perrine/Alamy Stock Photo; 16: Kryssia Campos/Moment/Getty Images; 17: JHVEPhoto/iStock/
Getty Images; 18: Stanislavs Vasilkovs/iStock/Getty Images; 19: Martin Harvey/The Image Bank/
Getty Images; 20: Paul Starosta/Stone/Getty Images; 21: (top) BrianLasenby/iStock/Getty Images,
(bottom) Alberthep/iStock/Getty Images; 22: Istvan Kadar Photography/Moment/Getty Images; 23:
daniilphotos/iStock/Getty Images; 24: Ken Griffiths/iStock/Getty Images; 25: Nick Ryden/500px/500Px
Plus/Getty Images; 26: Westhoff/iStock/Getty Images; 27: Westend61/Getty Images; 28: Mark Kostich/
iStock/Getty Images; 29: (top) Martin Harvey/The Image Bank/Getty Images, (bottom) Giulia
Fiori Photography/Moment/Getty Images; 30: (top) passion4nature/iStock/Getty Images, (bottom)
blickwinkel/A. Hartl/Alamy Stock Photo; 31: passion4nature/iStock/Getty Images; 32: (top) Michelle
Gilders/Alamy Stock Photo, (bottom) thomasmales/iStock/Getty Images; 33: Ryan M. Bolton/Alamy
Stock Photo; 34: passion4nature/iStock/Getty Images; 35: R. Andrew Odum/Photodisc/Getty Images;
36: Bill Draker/Rolfnp/Rolf Nussbaumer Photography/Alamy Stock Photo; 37: Michelle Gilders/Alamy
Stock Photo; 38: Vladimir_Krupenkin/iStock/Getty Images; 39: Craig Lovell/Corbis Documentary/
Getty Images; 40: Westend61/Getty Images; 41: (top) EcoPic/iStock/Getty Images, (bottom) Paul
Souders/Stone/Getty Images; 42: Tim Jackson/Photodisc/Getty Images; 43: (top) R. Andrew Odum/
Photodisc/Getty Images, (bottom) wrangel/iStock/Getty Images; 44: twildlife/iStock/Getty Images;
45: Mara Brandl/imageBROKER/Getty Images; 46: (top) princessdlaf/E+/Getty Images, (bottom) Joe
McDonald/The Image Bank/Getty Images; 47: EdwardSnow/iStock/Getty Images;
48: maikid/E+/Getty Images

Visit us online at penguinrandomhouse.com.

Library of Congress Cataloging-in-Publication Data is available.

Manufactured in China

ISBN 9780593522004 (pbk)   10 9 8 7 6 5 4 3 2 1 WKT
ISBN 9780593522011 (hc)   10 9 8 7 6 5 4 3 2 1 WKT

TOTALLY TURTLES!

by Ginjer L. Clarke

Sea turtles almost never leave the ocean. Land tortoises (say: TOR-tuss-ez) hardly ever go in

Variable mud turtle

the water. Other types of turtles swim in rivers and hide in mud.

Turtles have been around for millions of years, since the time of dinosaurs. Some tortoises live to be more than 100 years old! Turtles can survive in many types of habitats, or homes.

Olive ridley sea turtle

River cooter

How can turtles live for so long, in so many places? Let's explore where these amazing animals live and what they do.

Radiated tortoise

Sea Swimming

A female green sea turtle swims in the ocean all the time, except when she lays eggs on land. She crawls out of the water onto the beach. She has returned to where she was born.

The mother green sea turtle digs a hole. *Plop!* She slowly drops about 100 soft eggs into the hole, one by one. *Push!* Then she fills in the hole with sand and swims back into the sea. She does not return.

The sand protects her eggs from the sun and heat. But raccoons, coyotes, and foxes will eat the turtle eggs if they find a nest.

Two months later, the full moon lights up the sky. The baby green turtles have hatched out of their shells. But they are still buried under the sand.

Dig! Dig! The tiny turtles flap their flippers to break free. Suddenly, the sand sinks and a hole opens. They climb up and out. Then they race down the beach to the ocean. Baby sea turtles follow the light of the moon and stars on the water to know which way to go.

The baby turtles swim all night and the next day to get far away from the beach.

Baby green turtles float on beds of seaweed. They eat tiny crabs and shrimp. They have to watch out for hungry birds and fish that will eat them. Only one out of thousands of baby turtles hatched will live to be one year old. *Yikes!*

Young green turtles eat fish and
jellyfish. But adult green turtles eat
mostly sea grass and algae. This green
food makes the fat in their bodies green.
That is how green turtles got their name!

The hawksbill sea turtle is named for its birdlike beak. Like all turtles, it does not have teeth. But its sharp beak is perfect for catching and cutting up food.

Nip! A hawksbill turtle pokes its beak into a coral reef. *Rip!* It grabs a colorful sea sponge. It also eats shrimp and squid.

The hawksbill is a fast swimmer. It flaps its big flippers like bird wings. But it has to rest, too. This turtle can sleep underwater for hours. It hides under a rock so sharks and octopuses will not find it.

Most sea turtles like warm water. But the leatherback turtle has a thick layer of fat, so it can live in cold water. Its shell is darker and smoother than other sea turtles' shells. The leatherback is the largest of the seven types of sea turtles. It weighs up to 2,000 pounds!

Zoom! The leatherback can dive
deeper than other sea turtles. *Boom!*
It catches a jellyfish, its favorite food.
The leatherback is not hurt by the poison
in the jellyfish. This tough turtle also
has special spines to keep jellyfish from
slipping out of its mouth.

The olive ridley is the smallest sea turtle. It weighs up to 100 pounds. Its round, olive-green shell is about the size of a large pizza.

There are more olive ridleys than any other type of sea turtle. They are famous because female olive ridleys gather in large groups once a year. They lay their eggs together to give their babies a better chance of surviving.

Whoosh! Thousands of olive ridley turtles swarm a beach at night. *Swoosh!* They all dig holes, lay eggs, and swim away together. What an amazing event!

River Living

Red-eared sliders gather in groups, too. They climb onto a rock or a log in a river or a pond to get warm in the sun. Sometimes lots of sliders crowd onto a rock and stack on top of each other.

The sliders spot a snake! *Slide! Glide!* They slip into the river to hide. Sliders are named for how they move. They are called red-eared because of their red stripes. These marks help warn predators, but they are not ears. Turtles have ears inside their heads, not outside.

The painted turtle is also brightly colored. It has red, orange, and yellow shapes on its shell and stripes on its body. These colors warn raccoons, birds, and fish to keep away, just like the red-eared sliders' stripes.

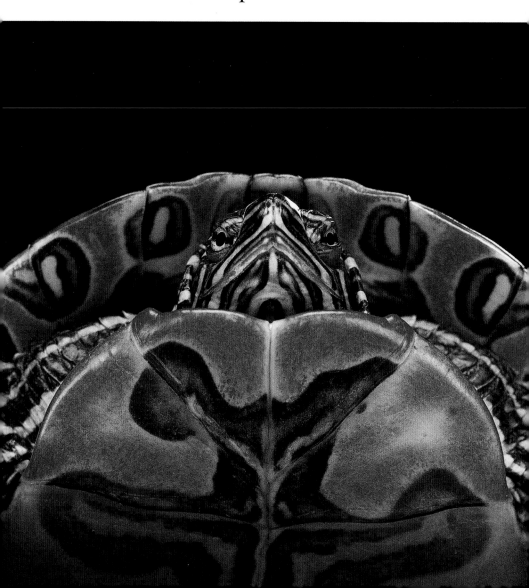

Painted turtles also bask in the sun together. Sometimes 50 turtles pile onto one log. *Danger!* They all plop into the river when they sense trouble. *Dive!* They also swim around eating plants. Painted turtles sleep on the bottom of the river at night and during winter.

Most river turtles can swim in water and walk on land to look for food. But the pig-nosed turtle can only swim. It is named for its piglike nose that works like a straw. It also has a soft shell and big flipper feet, so it swims like a sea turtle.

Snort! A pig-nosed turtle rises to the surface and breathes air. Then it dives back down. *Sniff!* It smells for food with its squishy nose. It finds a tasty snail. This turtle also eats fish, insects, plants, and ripe fruit that falls into the river.

The snake-necked turtle is the most common turtle in Australia. It belongs to the group of turtles called side-necked turtles. These turtles have to fold their long necks to the side to protect them. All other types of turtles can pull their necks inside of their shells.

This turtle hunts frogs, crabs, insects, and worms in a surprising way. *Stretch!* It pushes its long neck into an S shape. *Strike!* It springs forward close to a crab.

The snake-necked turtle opens its
mouth fast so water rushes in. The crab
is also sucked in. The turtle shuts it
mouth and traps the crab.

The yellow-spotted Amazon River turtle is also a side-necked turtle. Only the males and young turtles have bright yellow spots on their heads. The females are twice as big as the males, at up to two feet long. This makes them one of the biggest river turtles.

Crunch! Munch! Most river turtles eat animals, but the yellow-spotted turtle likes mostly plants. The Amazon River floods in the rainy season. Then this turtle can reach even more plants and fruits as the water level gets higher.

Mud Wading

The matamata lives in the Amazon River, too. But it stays on the muddy bottom. It hides using camouflage (say: KAH-meh-flazh) that helps it blend in.

This big turtle looks like a rock or a log while it sits still. Its triangle-shaped head has skin flaps, so it appears to be a fallen leaf. It is also covered in algae.

Fish do not see the matamata until it is too late. *Gulp!* The matamata sucks a fish into its mouth. *Slurp!* It sticks its snout out of the water like a straw to breathe. Then it goes back to hiding.

The Florida softshell turtle also has a little snout for breathing. But it gets air in another way, too—through its skin! A softshell turtle has thick skin instead of a hard shell.

Its shell is light and can bend. *Squeeze!* The softshell turtle jams its body under a rock. Then it mushes down into the mud, so only its neck and head stick out.

But it does not only hide. It fights back, too. *Snap!* The turtle bites an alligator that tries to eat it. Then it swims away quickly.

The alligator snapping turtle has a huge head and long tail covered in scales like an alligator. It does not fight off alligators like the softshell turtle, though. It eats them! The "snapper" is the world's largest freshwater turtle.

Wiggle, wiggle! A snapper moves a small, pink, wormlike bit in its mouth. Fish are attracted to it and swim close.

Chomp! The snapper bites the fish with its scissor-sharp jaws. It will eat anything it can catch, including fish, snakes, other turtles, and alligators.

33

The common musk turtle is small and does not swim much. Instead, it walks on the bottom of muddy rivers. It is hiding from hawks, eagles, fish, and alligators. But it can also defend itself.

A big fish tries to eat a musk turtle.
Pow! The turtle squirts out a gross-
smelling liquid called musk. This ability
gives the turtle the nickname "stinkpot."

The fish still does not back off. What
happens next? The little musk turtle bites
the big fish with its sharp beak. *Wow!*

The yellow mud turtle can make a stinky smell, too. But it usually tries to stay hidden. It hunts for insects, frogs, and lizards in a muddy pond. A mud turtle can smell food in the dark water. Its powerful jaws can even crush a snail.

In summer, the pond gets dry and hot. *Squish! Squoosh!* The mud turtle buries itself in the mud. It eats earthworms, spiders, and ticks to stay alive. It also stays in the mud all winter to keep warm.

Land Loving

Not all turtles live in water. *Tortoise* is the name for turtles that live on land. The Galápagos (say: guh-LAH-puh-gus) or giant tortoise is the largest in the world. It can weigh more than 500 pounds! It lives only on the Galápagos Islands in the Pacific Ocean.

The giant tortoise lives a long time, more than 100 years! That is because it sleeps a lot—about 16 hours per day.

Yawn! A giant tortoise wakes up from its nap. It moves *very* slowly, like all tortoises. But the giant tortoise is one of the slowest animals of all. Only sloths, snails, slugs, and starfish are slower!

Another large land lover is the
leopard tortoise. It has spots on its shell
like a leopard. It acts like the giant
tortoise. But it lives in many habitats,
including grasslands, deserts, and
mountains.

The leopard
tortoise makes a
lot of noises. *Grunt!*
Groan! Two males
bite and fight each
other to attract a
female. *Hiss!* The female
is annoyed. She pulls her head
and feet into her shell to hide from them.

The smallest tortoise is the speckled padloper. It is up to four inches long. Lots of animals try to eat this tiny tortoise. *Scoot!* It hides under rocks or plants to stay out of sight and to escape the hot sun.

The pancake tortoise is small, too. Its shell is flat and soft like a pancake, so it fits in tight places. *Sploot!* It can squeeze between rocks. It uses its spiky legs to hold on tightly so an attacker cannot pull it out.

Scritch! Scratch! A desert tortoise uses its feet like shovels to dig a burrow. It needs a cool place to get out of the hot desert sun. It stays in its burrow for months to avoid the summer heat.

Sometimes two male desert tortoises fight. *Flip!* One tortoise pushes the other. *Flop!* It falls onto its back. The fallen tortoise hurries to turn over. It could die from the sun and heat if it gets stuck.

Many turtles can pull their head and legs inside their shells for safety. But the common box turtle has a special shell.

A dog comes close to sniff a box turtle. The turtle quickly pulls its body inside its shell. *Shut!* Then it closes the bottom part of its shell tightly like a box. The dog swats at the box turtle, but the dog cannot get inside.

The turtle's soft body is protected from almost all danger. Sometimes its shell gets hurt on the outside. But this special shell can even fix itself. *What?!*

Turtles are truly amazing creatures. They live on almost every part of our planet. They take their homes with them on their backs. And they can survive all kinds of trouble. They are totally cool!